Successfully

Demands Six Things!

great success

EMMANUEL MUDI

Copyright

Effectively requests six Things.
Chapter 1
1.Clear objectives are crucial.
Versatility and learning.
Measurable Progress
Successful Objective Setting.
Chapter 2
2.Relentlessness is fundamental.
WHY IS BEING Relentless So Intense?
How would you develop relentlessness?
PRIORITIZE ACTIVITIES.
Industriousness is equivalent to achievement.
Keeping up with Tenacious Exertion.
Chapter 3
3.Consistent learning is vital.
How might nonstop learning help me?
Profession improvement.
Fostering an attitude of learning

Chapter 4
4.Flexibility is critical.
Improving Flexibility.
Chapter 5
5.Connections are basic.
Developing significant connections.
Chapter 6
6.Balance is fundamental.
Vital: taking care of oneself.
A contextual investigation into equilibrium.
Conclusion

Effectively requests six Things.

Different people have different definitions of success. But most of the time, it means fully utilizing one's personal and professional potential and achieving meaningful, worthwhile goals that are in line with one's values. Achievement is a continuous course of development as opposed to a proper endpoint, as individuals' objectives and values will generally change over their lives. While intricate, six key components give the establishment to essentially every example of overcoming adversity.

Chapter 1

1.Clear objectives are crucial.

Progress is unthinkable without clarity on goals. Thus, the main basic element for progress lies in consistently characterizing substantial objectives. For example, "I need achievement" needs particularity. In contrast, "I will join Company X within a year" sets a specific goal.

Defining clear objectives is a key stage in our personal growth. This permits us to get ready and remain focused on the particular objectives we look for. Putting forth clear objectives provides us with a feeling of motivation and worthwhileness we need to accomplish the fantasies we aim for. That being said, the following are the six motivations behind why laying out clear objectives is fundamental for self-awareness and advancement:

. Course and concentration.

Clear objectives give us an internal compass and motivation in our lives. They can assist us with recognizing where we need to go and what we need to accomplish. In the event that we don't set clear objectives, we could float carelessly, deficient with regards to a sense of direction and concentration throughout everyday life. Our goals give us the focus we need to put everything we have into making our dreams come true. The more we foster our bearing and concentration, the more pre-arranged we are in attempting to keep our objectives straight.

Versatility and learning.

Objectives give us an open door to learn and adjust. We will unavoidably experience setbacks or unexpected events. Nonetheless, defining clear objectives permits us to change our methodology, look for new techniques, and keep advancing toward our goals.

Finding changes and improvements that can help us achieve our objectives is the primary focus of adaptability. Putting forth objectives expects us to try, permitting us to advance in the meantime. Since there is a process for achieving any goal, adaptability and knowledge are essential life skills.

Measurable Progress

Objectives are quantifiable. This will permit us to monitor our advancement and sort out the kinds of enhancements required. Estimating our advancement gives us a feeling of achievement, which will assist us in remaining on track. However, it will assist us in commending the victories en route. As we attempt and arrive at our objectives, consider quantifiable advancement designated spots toward what we previously cultivated. As we complete every designated spot, we continue onward, permitting us to adhere to our advancement toward that particular ultimate objective.

Successful Objective Setting.

All around-figured-out objectives have particular characteristics: they are precise, quantifiable, doable, pertinent, and time-bound. Observing objective advancement through slug journaling or applications supports responsibility and inspiration. Notwithstanding, objectives may work with progress assuming that they match intrinsic interests and values rather than outer benchmarks.

At the point when Amelia put forth the express objective of sending off her visual depiction business, it drove her whole achievement venture. At first scared, she separated it into more modest achievements, such as making a portfolio site and pitching five expected month-to-month clients. Meeting these goals kept her on target until she signed three long-haul contracts in 13 months or less.

Chapter 2

2.Relentlessness is fundamental.

What is Relentlessness?

As indicated by the Oxford Word reference, relentlessness is characterized as "the quality or reality of having the option to solidly grasp something."

What Relentlessness is Essential to Business Visionaries?

As I'm certain you've found in your pioneering venture, there are numerous gleaming articles competing for your focus. What's more, since business visionaries embrace attempting new things, it's not difficult to become derailed and occupied by every one of the open doors that come your way.

From promoting strategies to beginning new lines of business, bouncing from one thing to another can immediately turn into a catastrophe waiting to happen. You should be determined and cautious with your activities, so you don't lose hold of your vision.

WHY IS BEING Relentless So Intense?

Excitedness and anxiety are two mental states that entrepreneurs frequently experience. In light of this, you probably experience times when you are doing "everything" to attempt to transform your thought into reality or stop an issue.

At the point when you are beginning your business, you might endeavor to happily take advantage of each system administration chance you experience to develop your image of mindfulness. While this system, in principle, is perfect, in actuality, it can remove you from other fundamental undertakings you should deal with.

At the point when your business is leveling or battling, you might make a pass at all the promotion choices to attempt and madly create income. Yet, without an essential methodology, all that energy and monetary result is unproductive.

It isn't difficult to continue through to the end.

We live in a time where we have a staggering amount of data and amazing open doors readily available, so remaining on track amidst everything is significant. Relinquish FOMO and have the solidarity to stay with your arrangement and own it.

Try not to let what others are doing send you off track.

How would you develop relentlessness?

The following are four basic steps from Entrepreneur.com's article, "Why Industriousness is One of the Most Critically Disregarded Innovative Abilities," to develop diligence.

Put forth objectives.

You want to understand what you are clutching, so get some margin to put forth clear objectives. Without knowing where you are going, you will be easily diverted.

PRIORITIZE ACTIVITIES.

Objectives are your endpoint; propensities get you there. Since you never really have command over the results of your objectives, you want to concentrate every day to move towards them. Transform your activity ventures into propensities!

I love your work.

I don't 100 percent concur with this tip, on the grounds that occasionally I figure love can dazzle (in connections and business). Be that as it may, when you love what you do, you are bound to clutch it.

Encircle yourself with diligent individuals.

You are who you surround yourself with, so develop a circle of steady, engaged, and driven individuals. You'll be astounded at the amount of effect this possesses on your capacity to keep with it and finish things.

Industriousness is equivalent to achievement.

Tenacity is a trait shared by the most successful entrepreneurs. They battle through the unavoidable difficult stretches with earnestness and industriousness. They establish objectives, develop a strategy, carry it out on a daily basis, and maintain a network of like-minded companions. In this way, the lesson of the story is: clutch what you trust and own it!

NEED Backing?

At times, it's difficult to be aware, assuming your vision and objectives are practical and reachable. Book a free business training meeting to talk through your objectives, thoughts, and difficulties!

While objectives give guidance, constant exertion and coarseness depict the mentality and outlook important to accomplish objectives in spite of difficulties. Most examples of overcoming adversity include gigantic ingenuity, including many bombed examinations or turns. Predictable routine activities like appearance up recognize those ready to stay with long-haul points.

Keeping up with Tenacious Exertion.

Maintaining tenacity necessitates avoiding burnout and stagnation. This means exerting unwavering effort in a strategic manner, working hard, and not obsessing over outcomes or exercising unhealthy overexertion. Involving difficulties as criticism and celebrating little wins fabricates strength to persevere while confronting obstacles.

Jenna, a yearning business visionary, showed ironclad steadiness by awakening at 5 a.m. every day to chip away at her internet-based business for a considerable length of time in spite of her first negligible pay. Her assurance assisted her with deliberately testing different items and showcasing strategies without losing trust, resulting in a six-figure leap forward.

Chapter 3

3.Consistent learning is vital.

Having a learning mindset makes it easier to continue growing, which is essential for long-term success, while goals and perseverance form the foundation. Two elements empower long-lasting learning: abilities to accept and gifts can improve instead of staying fixed and focusing on gathering information through conventional instruction, mentorship, preparation, or self-study to fabricate abilities.

Persistent learning is the method involved with procuring new abilities and information constantly over the long haul (or 'upskilling'). This assists you with creating, both actually and expertly, new ways to open doors and accomplish your maximum capacity.

You could likewise hear the term 'deep-rooted realization', which is a comparable idea but typically alludes to self-awareness instead of business-related improvement.

Constant and long-lasting learning can take a wide range of forms; everybody advances in an unexpected way. From night classes at your neighborhood college to bitesize learning or online courses, you can propel your range of abilities and move past your present place of employment.

How might nonstop learning help me?

There are a scope of advantages to persistent picking up, including:

Acquiring certainty. With the information that you've acquired extra abilities to take you forward in your vocation, you will feel more prepared to take on difficulties or new open doors.

Profession improvement.

Acquiring new abilities can prompt future advancements or expansions beyond your present place of employment. It makes you more significant to your ongoing manager and more attractive to planned businesses, assuming you're between occupations; constant learning shows that you are focused on really buckling down, bettering yourself, and remaining applicable in the business.

Getting or refreshing your capabilities and certificates. In your work, you might have to do normal preparation to accomplish or refresh declarations or certain capabilities; constant learning can assist you with remaining focused and state-of-the-art.

Having a significant impact on your point of view. Your perspectives and attitudes can shift as you learn. Ceaseless learning can provide you with a more prominent comprehension of issues you could seem to be, as well as assist you with taking care of issues that you were unable to see a response to previously.

Helping efficiency. Feeling satisfied and certain prompts a lift in efficiency, which is likewise an advantage for bosses. Both the success of a business and the length of time that employees remain employed can be affected by this.

Empowering others. Assuming you lead by example by showing that learning is significant, you could rouse people around you to foster their own abilities further. This could, thus, further develop your workplace.

Instances of constant and deep-rooted learning.

Formal and informal methods can be used for continuous or lifelong learning. Courses from colleges and universities, outside workshops and conferences, and online instruction are all examples of formal learning.

Fostering an attitude of learning

Mastering ever-evolving fields is made easier by a few best practices: reflecting through journaling, remaining strongly inquisitive instead of confident, and presenting oneself to different suppositions. Individual drive and cleverness eventually describe deep-rooted students who effectively level up their skills.

For instance, Arthur was able to avoid stagnation in his career by enrolling in a rigorous coding boot camp while he was working full-time. By embracing advancing as a way of life rather than a task, he acquired sufficient mastery to change into a product designer job in 2 years through nonstop self-schooling.

Chapter 4

4.Flexibility is critical.

Success comes to those who are able to adapt to the world's overwhelming changes. While steadiness fixates on keeping up with exertion notwithstanding outer fluctuation, versatility alludes to interior adaptability in techniques, systems, or jobs to suit advancing conditions better. Versatile individuals exhibit deftness in adjusting their methodology, propensities, or capabilities to line up with evolving conditions. This distinguishes them from unbending people who do exactly the same things, paying little mind to results.

Improving Flexibility.

Supporting flexibility starts by observing automatic responses to change while taking on a development outlook. Moreover, differing encounters, difficulties, and even disappointments sharpen abilities to properly tailor reactions. Individuals' ability to explore, feel awkward, and fundamentally self-evaluate permits versatility to turn out to be natural.

For Tina, consistent profession shifts as jobs quickly digitize typified flexibility. By proactively upskilling herself while relinquishing uneasiness-based responses to transform, she turned from conventional promotion to computerized showcasing supervisor to man-made intelligence expert for more than 10 years, demonstrating flexibility that empowers perseverance through accomplishment.

Chapter 5

5.Connections are basic.

"No man is an island whole of itself." Artist John Donne's ageless words reasonably capture how powerful connections are for individual and expert achievement. From offering close-to-home help and versatility to opening entryways of chance, encircling oneself with positive networks makes achievement attempts possible.

Developing significant connections.

While systems administration today infers trading business cards at gatherings, significant connections require a genuine association. That implies rehearsing liberality without anticipating quick returns, building bonds around normal interests or values, and sustaining common getting—not taking advantage of exchanges—to solidify connections that help enduring achievement.

A crucial relationship with her strange creative coach fitness set Melanie, a side-interest painter, on the way to turning into an acclaimed style originator. By utilizing this help and a few fortunate client associations, Melanie naturally built an organization that enhanced acknowledgment of her gifts until her particular prints became runway sensations.

Chapter 6

6.Balance is fundamental.

With limited day-to-day mental data transfer capacity, nothing subverts achievement quicker than ignoring this reality. Therefore, holistic self-care in the mental, emotional, and physical realms is the sixth essential foundation for success. Endeavoring to support execution while running on void definitely sets off the body's defensive systems to forestall burnout.

Vital: taking care of oneself.

While breaks reestablish efficiency, the deeper aim behind balance lies in focusing on by and large health, not exclusively achievement. That might include getting satisfactory rest, keeping up with social ties, taking part in leisure activities, practicing consistently, or eating nutritious food varieties, among other taking care of oneself strategies. What are powerful equilibrium shifts in light of individual prerequisites?

Ravi exemplified the heavenly use of equilibrium as a multi-enthusiastic business visionary. In spite of a serious responsibility, he depends on rehearsals like morning reflection, enjoying little reprieves at regular intervals, adhering to family suppers daily, and totally turning off one day week after week. Ravi accepts that this routine has empowered him to support his business accomplishments for a really long time without huge wellbeing outcomes.

A contextual investigation into equilibrium.

Jeremy was a climbing business chief who constrained himself to succeed. However, he ascended the stepping stool quickly from the get-go; huge work pressure and a nonexistent balance between fun and serious activities incurred significant damage by his mid-30s. Jeremy lost interest in his career and developed chronic insomnia, back pain, and irritability.

However, Jeremy finally decided to make self-care a priority after receiving a wake-up call regarding an emergency health situation. He started leaving the workplace before, took customary excursions, detached totally from work, declined unnecessary tasks, and, surprisingly, began treatment. Continuously, Jeremy recovered mental and close-to-home harmony as his way of life balance moved along.

Subsequently, his vocation reignited into his most useful and imaginative period. Jeremy immovably thinks that laying out economic equilibrium empowered him to rediscover professional achievement, but this time based on his conditions without compromising health. His experience demonstrates that taking care of oneself can fuel proficient achievement as opposed to hindering it.

Key action items

Obviously characterized objectives lined up with interests and values give fundamental bearing to really channel endeavors.

Steadiness epitomized by resolute tirelessness and restrained consistency creates fuel to overcome deterrents in transit to progress.

A learning mindset necessitates proactive self-education and supports continuous development by enhancing competencies to distinguish oneself in changing domains.

Supporting adaptability, spryness, and quick course amendment, flexibility is a basic strength for persevering through importance and effect.

Sustaining strong networks puts forth solo achievement attempts conceivable through outstanding organization impacts, conveying constant reassurance and unforeseen open doors.

Key taking care of oneself powers maximized operation by forestalling burnout and sustaining all-encompassing wellbeing across mental, profound, and actual domains.

While addresses about intense dreams might ignite beginning inspiration, just incorporating these six fundamental fixings—clear objectives, determined exertion, ceaseless learning, areas of strength for versatility, and equilibrium—changes sparkles into enduring triumph. Consequently, true achievement requires both longing and a sincere obligation to these essential support points.

Conclusion

Those encountering significant achievement have moved past inspiration or motivation alone. Devoted consolidation of the six nonnegotiable fundamentals framed here lays out the designs, frameworks, and mentalities empowering constancy, development, and local area to flourish. While the particulars of the excursion differ decisively between people, these fundamental structure blocks remain basically all-inclusive.

Hence, as you progress toward fantastic objectives, recall that secluded endeavors never crawl toward victory. Enduring accomplishment requires coordinating clear objectives, eager exertion, nonstop learning, versatility to change, steady networks, and taking care of oneself for balance. How have these six essential components been incorporated into your success plan? The first step toward completing your unique success puzzle is honest self-assessment.

www.ingramcontent.com/pod-product-compliance
Lightning Source LLC
Chambersburg PA
CBHW070848310526
45796CB00014B/287